Such Common Stories

Lawrence Hopperton

En Route Books and Media, LLC
Saint Louis, MO

⊕ *ENROUTE*
Make the time

En Route Books and Media, LLC

5705 Rhodes Avenue

St. Louis, MO 63109

contact@enroutebooksandmedia.com

Cover Credit: Sebastian Mahfood

Copyright 2022 Lawrence Hopperton

ISBN-13: 978-1-956715-70-5

LCCN: 2022941986

There is one story and one story only
That will prove worth your telling,
Whether as learned bard or gifted child;
To it all lines or lesser gauds belong
That startle with their shining
Such common stories as they stray into.

- Robert Graves, "To Juan at the Winter Solstice"

Acknowledgements

Some of these poems have appeared in *The Agape Review*, *Panoply*, *Sweetycat Press*, *Lummox Press*, *Poets 88*, and *The Poet*.

I would like to give special thanks to Andrew Brooks. He has read almost all the poetry I have ever written, provided constant encouragement and, more importantly, a considered, critical response that has always led to improvement.

I would also like to thank my publisher, Dr. Sebastian Mahfood, OP, of En Route Books & Media. Our relationship began as academics in the field of online learning and founding members of the Faith-based Online Learning Directors association. From there it grew, and poetry came creeping in. This is my second book of poems with Sebastian, following *Table for Three* (2021).

Table of Contents

Introduction

When I started my academic journey at Ottawa University some time ago, little did I realize that the direction of my life would radically change because of poetry. Yes, poetry. I was firmly charted towards a career in science and yet, as fate would have it, the university required science majors to take one or two English classes. I opted for an evening class in poetry that was taught by a PhD student who looked more like a lumberjack than a professor—he simply sat on a desk facing us, cracked open a massive book of poetry (all the greats), and began reading. I was intrigued (okay, spellbindingly hooked) by the existential nature of the poems and the quest for meaning(s). At the end of the semester, I quickly signed up for a second poetry class. There was something about poetic words and how they touched the soul that I had never experienced in dissecting Drosophila melanogaster (fruit flies) for genetic experiments. As you might have guessed, I switched majors. Poetry truly changed the course of my life.

Therefore, it was with gratitude and great pleasure that my path crossed with that of Dr. Lawrence Hopperton. We shared an interest in literary studies, theological reflection, online learning, and, at the time of our meeting, the deep loss of someone unspeakably dear in our respective lives. As our friendship grew, I became aware of a secret trove of poetry that Larry had written over his life and, to my delight, was continuing to write. I asked him if I could read some. On numerous occasions I would be honoured by Larry making a pilgrimage to our place in Waterloo, ON (or alternatively me to his) to hear him read some of the poetry he was working on. Over an evening coffee and sometimes a later dram we would read his poems and talk poetry.

His words then, as now in *Such Common Stories*, convey(ed) a rugged earthiness that resonates with those who love nature, the land, the creature/Creator dance, and the community around us. In this latest book, our senses awaken to a world we often miss— life captured among the everchanging seasons draws us into discovering the profound

within the common and what we might
hurriedly mislabel the mundane. As I have
come to know Larry, these poems are surely
rooted in his life. Yet, his poetry beckons all
of us manner that says, "These are *your*
common stories too." The swath is inclusive,
broadly inviting—none are left behind.

Dr. William (Bill) J. Webb
Tyndale University

Zen garden no. 1

belly swell outline
scopes on a pencil background
knobs twist you alive

      and the branches twist
      alive and snow melts recede
      freeze again tonight

seedlings shrug winter
spruce skirts weighted down waiting
for chipmunks to come

      it's coming and swells
      hope and ground squirrel and we
      wait coffee at the door

Straight and ready

We raked the first drop
up to the fences, off the deck
out of the garden. Harvest what's left
then cut the stalks. Pots in the shed
with the garden furniture
the barbeque. Is the gas off?

Little leaves are everywhere.
The next rake will be maples
then wait for the oak holdouts,
for the first snow on this
soon cocooned
until the green sun.

Ouimet Canyon

Gone green breeze and warm nights.
The sun follows to find itself south.
Insect hums, phoebe calls migrated.
Ouimet and clouds tumble evergreen
tips. There is scent – snow and rain drops
across the earth-gap spill
a black face. The walls sink
the boulder floor. A pillar rises

rim-high and a raven rides the current
cries echo wall-to-wall, and a straggler
digs a last grub out. The land forgets
and sleeps let our little-blood
pile the wood we scavenged
to feed our fire and huddle close.

Wind blow

red cheek bedtime
lullaby prayer fights
lights out sleep now
I love you

shuts down outside
snow and drifting
the shed the car
closed and dark

breath listens
the spruce bends
maple ash bone black
and the wind blows

Taliesin's first thanksgiving

settles in cold satin-lined coats
on our shoulders; insulated walls
separate the afternoon fading
skies mirror the bay to its depth.
We harvested beets and carrots
to preserve in foundational dirt

and the woodpile stacked shoulder high.
The stove sparks sap and heats cabin
corners, cooks turkey; dishes clatter
wash-water warmed in pots,
cools. The radio distorts
draughts across the floor.

Our little one in sleepers with feet
cries, finds mama, and hugs a face.
She understands this evening
and tonight, there will be stars,
leaves down gravel roads rustle marshes
 migrate rock slopes red and white

windswept ground carved
knuckle-deep petroglyphs.
An outboard motor drones away.

Pine trunks twisting cliffs, acorn hands
clenched in pockets. Our shoulders
our knees squeeze our bodies small

pause a moment, our noses run
unbuttressed water-coloured
oil-lit tables seat twenty-five,
give thanks for cider and pied
windows with spider frost and breath
between resolve and darkness.

Escarpment

Fall was only coming until maple
even oak holds stripped bare. It rained.

Then it stopped. Then hail wind
whipped our bottom-up fire high

dark underfoot, dusting frost, rock
spine and caves fissure down.

It's lonely at the end. Cut the chill.
Smoke November: layer up, layer down

prune the wild rose packed in compost
bags at the curb, melting trilliums.

Red fickle

Snow on the back porch
driveways wait out the storm

this morning hair, eyes lift
distracting filaments down

tantalized finger-scented soap
icicles drip smiles and eyes

this advent skin promise
whispers hide inside and child

bare temperature poinsettia
fickle winter

Watershed

April skies drive shafts of light
into winter. The whole earth heaves
old cold away and brown land breathes,
swelling underfoot. The last snow

patches shrink into shades
hidden between rocks. Old ice cracks,
shifts to the far ends of lakes. Creeks
bloat, flow. Streams rush to high cascades.

A first fresh wind blows a light tune
through wide skies over long lakes, crowds
the hollow sound and heavy clouds
out of the air. No scent but soon.

Too early for new shoots but sap stirs
pines and the mountain trees will bud
birch-tips as red as blood
chipmunks feel the twist of hunger.

Lowlands see evening fume
red across the heights of the shield
on this plateau. Farms burn their fields
To ash. The tundra will bloom.

Limbo

Twelve degrees crystal the surface
all the way down drains snowman
monoliths into crocuses begin.

Spring crops should be good.
Standard time. Hawks crest low
adjust the air lifting currents. Coons

tuft earth against the south wall.
The earth breaks under receding
children laughing down the street

rain boots resurrected, coat-sleeves
tied at the waist in this
red moon tonight.

Pivot

It could be accepting that
leaf-bud dappled trillium sprints.
Bulbs break ground like tulips.
Annuals root. Outcomes swirl in
honeysuckle yellow, red and free
a red falcon and a falconer.

Regrets are leaves we didn't rake
under the snow- mouse
shelters, bugs, and fences
coons forage. Earth warms chipmunks
past the cat at the sun-deck door
waiting for iced tea.

Winter camp

Weather works against us.
We might get there but
could we get back? Moose

Burgundian for 12 cooked
yesterday, sampled and it feeds
leftovers if you are still hungry.

Winter camp with video games
a fireplace in the family room. Dig the cat
out of the basement. Move stuff

dad keeps. She wants to play. She likes
games. Take the '68 Camaro
but make it red. There are logs

from the garage on the fire.
Short night, shorter morning.

Taliesin says goodnight

the time is right
still is the night
our fire is light
with a song and a whistle

dance for the fire
everyone's desire
a marshmallow choir
with a song and a whistle

we listen and sight
stretches to night
revealing starlight
with a song and a whistle

and good night.

Camp Daigle

For Marg and Frank

I

It's high water even before spring
culverts flood the road erodes either
side, ice in the middle, potholes. Snapping

turtles will nest here. Now pressure cracks
the ice like this cold snap. Even sap
stopped running. We collected 60

liters in plastic jugs these last weeks.
40 to 1 like water from trees.
Boil it down to its secret syrup.

This morning, our eyes closed, tiptoed
around sleeping bags, stoked the wood
     stove.
chopped wood outside and built a boiling

maple morning day, this afternoon
snow-toffee twisting-sticks, sample this

time. Camp rule. Stay off the lake, out of
    caves.

II

You planned this a year out, didn't tell;
hurried ahead. Made sure it's Ok
back to the birch. Wait for Dorothy

awe, an emerald cliff, a horse-cart
mine, radiation like a pocket watch,
fissured and fractured. Our footstep

gobsmacks and baby fingers explore
the rock face, find samples for geiger
counters and watches from the '40s.

We cower. The icicle mouth snaps
and falls on our ducked backs. Call them out
all tired. The syrup boiled all day

down, now 5 degrees above water boiling
at this altitude. Tomorrow morning
pancakes with bacon and fried potatoes.

Ben is gone

The escarpment raises its spine and dives
just north of the rain last night
drives dark down ice roads

snow-banked either side.
They have always told the story here:
Big Bay Ben opens the channel,

breaks winter with horned
spines under pressure spots
just off White Cloud Island,

40 meters long, horns on its head
diamond and fire eyes glow
the night-ice. Scouts have seen it

from Camp Charl'bro. It's recorded.
A newspaper article framed in '64
hangs near the woodstove in the meeting
    house

with a kitchen, outhouses in the cold
crack the black back. Don't take long.
Morning will have coffee and leaders talk.

You will wake up in cold sleeping cabins
with the song for 16-year-olds we have not
        sung
since this morning, twice round the
        campsite

walking and slipping; more footing with
        snow
under the crust. The pines are birch
overcast background expansions

you feel in your spine this end time
clears the channel breaks
thunders visceral pressure

ridges thrust up calves and thighs
ripple this spartan landscape.
Ben is gone now, down the escarpment.

Tomato and frangipani

The subway exits at the post office.
Stores grow flowers to the curb
geraniums, pansies, herbs we
step around in boots.

I want to grow tomatoes.
Apartment windows are violets
and frangipani stalks nursed
through winter, ferns beside

azalea side tables, showers
splash coriander scented skin.
Frangis don't like night air
sleep. Coffee tomorrow.

Birth of Venus

It's an ordinary day like Tuesday
in March or Sunday hawk circles.
It moves, it rustles driving charcoal
lines through fields. Groundswell
pools in most. Furrows wait.
Wind breaks as naked as it feels

down Main St. with nothing open.
Park ice softens, recedes underfoot.
Aphrodisia has awakened
the first geese in this Botticelli
heart beneath covered
breasts, covered mons.

Zen garden no. 2

a rabbit nibbles grass
at our afternoon tea-time
sensing a waiting

      the weeds are buried
      compost praying potato
      leaves and raspberries

when you plant maples
think next year will leaf
between daffodil shelters

      mum and dad are here
      little one with stormy eyes
      closed warm our cuddle

Samdog

A dog is a mash, an infant
mewling play positions
across the bed, nuzzling tonight
in my ear my shoulders your

nails my skin. Everything laughs.
Let me feed your morning eyes,
your mouth. Your fast feet
follow coffee, the floor, shuffle

and paw majestic instancy.
I shelter your muzzle.
scratch your neck and trust
my hand in your mouth.

Pangur Ban, my cat

> *I and Pangur Ban my cat,*
> *'Tis a like task we are at*
> *Hunting mice is his delight*
> *Hunting words I sit all night*
> 8th-century Irish marginalia

Hump your body, your tail
across my head. Settle. Eat.

I am bigger than you
up the stairs, between posts

down your belly your legs,
pick you up, cuddle your escape

away or come back perhaps
behind the refrigerator, the ceiling

in the mud room or dance our hind
feet between the sheets, rubbing faces.

Estate auction

I

Things collect space on shelves
dust in cupboards because Auntie Jen
found an estate auction in 1921.

Treasures passed this long
way relics, porcelain gypsies
dance around urns packed

with towels marked "Fragile"
with provenance refinished
and family embellishment.

II

We had an arrangement:
everything parks in the basement
because it's there, family barbeques

for the next few years and parcel
afternoons in boxes with names
in the basement. It can wait here a while.

auctioneers dragged her home
to the front yard for the high bidder.
She didn't know what sold that day

but missed treasured pieces collected and
          saved
stacks and pieces of silver services,
with unknown signatures,

report cards from daguerreotype
people with names before we were born.
They are here but and retirement comes.

III

Accents are interesting
but have no place. Here's a box:
cards and letters dated childhood

places packed up. Memories
considered to be sure.
Everything else laid out

for the auctioneer's song
the rest for charity
or recycle or landfill.

IV

We wake with coffee and folk
music on Saturday morning

gentle like letters from parents.

We will be gone to history soon:
after lunch, Elmira bids away
darlings and other things.

Your eyes say, "but the rent."
Just pretend. Our hurricane
lanterns flicker diamond moments.

The embarrassment
of Sierra Escumbre

I

The hills are as brown as March
            break sun,
as warm as home is cold. Muscles relax.
The catamaran shifts our weight. Trade
winds blaze our hair, our laughter away.

This resort is built with concrete slabs
like houses without dollars. You sketch
garzas - like herons, but smaller. They strut
the beach front of the bar and come close

out of reach. Feral cats in manicured brush
outside the dining room trust touristas.
Coconuts fall. It's casual here. All inclusive,
bathing suits and bars and food.

You draw your hair behind your ear,
sunset on your face, your eyes,
a cross around your neck
home with me from classes like the day war

rose and tried to forget my mother
afraid to send us to school.

We could end up dead under desks
like we were taught to keep us busy.

II

The mountains are not too far away-
a morning excursion and back by bus.
El Nicho at the top, spring fed, and falls
into pools stepping down.

I will stand guard while you get ready
A cave for a change room.
Forest lunch on the way down,
music and artists look for pesos

a dog looks for food, gives a lick.
My forearm pushes his throat away.
Pico San Juan is the highest. A tower
watches for storms that don't come.

It's a seven- year drought. Maybe one
hurricane each year. Emaciated cattle
on the roadside can't be killed. It's
crime. You are careful making the
            cow sign

warning cars or bicycles,
horses or donkeys salvaged
like car wheels, drawn to tourists

in the middle of the road.

Closed rooms get hot in the morning,
draw the sea up to our calves, with iced
            coffee.
Filippe and I talk about our daughters.
I brush sand off my legs. It tastes salt.

He hides in the brush for moments.
"Policia don't care about you – you bring
money. We don't bother touristas.
But we are friends. I give you a bracelet.

You give me a tee-shirt, a burger
is free for you. My wife, my little one,
Money is only a few weeks. Then nothing.
Fidel good. Raoul not so much. I get you cigars."

Caribbean squats on hopes- some pesos
maybe a package from Canada sometime.
I promise softness for children, an old man
on a porch, even if it's not true. Tomorrow
he will hide behind this tree.
Bathing skin stretched across the beach.
You and I swim with dolphins, tan
and tonight we sleep on a plane home.

The great conjunction

Gardens map future
seedlings high as your hand
bulbs under another snowfall.

It receded today, not completely.
Dark days step through renew
and branches snap. Tonight snaps

an advent, a great conjunction.
Solstice sunset east
for warm afternoons

Back to Ptolley Bay

The ferry docks and daylight drifts
reddens twilight umber stretching.

Are you surprised? My backpack
tapping your door open arms wide.

I knew your come-back promise
and I saw you in town twice yesterday.

Your hair, sharp air, your skin flushed taut
envelopes our lamp and casual talk

with tea and cheese, honey finger
tips touch warm welcomes.

Taliesin in the skate park

sun white, sun red
wilting and it's humid
on and on all day sunburned
shoulders, noses sweat.

Thunder closes but not much
not yet. Your overslept devil
drives you to the skate park
green sucking into yourself

and you laugh with roots
bursting the swale run
off gardens in sunshine
need more waves

and cloud covers. It's too cool
too exciting really.

Ultrasound

It's coming – the belly outline
scoped on a dull background

pencil sketched knobs and branches
twisting. Alive yet? We are waiting.

Snow on the porch again. That bare
temperature can wait, poinsettias fade

the driveway waits the storm out
this morning. This afternoon icicles

smile and eye this advent skin
and imagine promises whisper

hide inside and child. Wear your coat.
Wind flecks cold grey blue around

the windshield past the clock tower
on Main Street snowmen are dolmen

left over. It's coming, into this
foreground, the car seat, face wipes.

Snow melts. The patio recedes ice
overhangs before freeze-up tonight

Zen garden no. 3

wrestle tulips high
the house will hide our private
moments and shadow

      a glade and woodpile
      stacked and ready for winter
      filters light through trees

it is a talking point
over coffee or perhaps
french fries tomorrow

Rehearsing ordination

A door is a metaphor:
inside outside either side,
hanging curtains, or oak, glass
both sides: this and the other.

I am the camera setting
the stage, humming hymns
rehearsed a minute ago, position
light, sound, video checks and

action: music, ordination robes
clergy robes, a supplicant
accepts orders, stained-glass
arrays revealing light.

Two or more

1. Private chapel

Picture someone like a pope
in prayer, a tiny chapel.
Altar servers murmur latin

robes raised in personal praise.
We did that in choir school.
We recited the responses

didn't know what they meant
but could participate at the feet
of a meditative moment.

2. Morning prayer

Summer Sunday shine
sweat to the porch doors, to
the narthex greeting friends.
Where is the priest, the process?

Hymns with bits of choir scattered
through the congregation chanting
in old-style: prayer and readings,

a sermon partially scripted

testimonies our chosen
chants in thin alto we answer
with summer gusto
and the organ plays us out

side the sanctuary. We linger.
We talk together.

3.   Morningsong

Spiders seek boundaries
transitions tether
and triangulate structure

grow gossamer fat forests
with sunscreen and naps
swim to the island and back.

Search for wood. Cut the length
and stomp it. I will teach you to
tinder and kindle with games

and saw stories, and rouse
tomorrow with a morning song

perhaps this one.

4.   First Sunday after Covid

Capacity is limited to 25 percent
and the sacristy is as full as that.
Livestream works. The piano
prelude picks up well.

Our pastor processes to a soloist,
a cantor waiting for her time
at a distant peace. Prayer
and real people to respond

to this first communion.
The chalice is re-silvered.
Isolation ends with sanitizer
space between pews. We are

one voice humming through masks.
It's good to praise with people.

5. Maundy Thursday

Can you read Psalm 22 tonight?
The tenor has Covid
no time to prepare
just read it over there.

But now rehearse the hymns and anthems
our shaky parish quartet sings
up the aisle to the podium.
Drop the page. Adjust the mic

test and begin. It's a psalm
a poem and the spirit on me
speaks this Gethsemane
redemption on the web.

A joyful noise

Valentin never plays piano.
It's just a vehicle
he hears through fingers
and echoes and
teaches us to sing

like Russian opera:
'shout artistically
open throat and support
focus through forehead'
in broken English

directed with an eyebrow
a nose dip, nod the head.
We get it.
We are instruments.
He brought me to sing

like Christ's last words
alone or a Gregorian choir
brings the congregation
to unison, then
silence erupts.

The annual church plant sale

I stood in my bare feet on the grass
and drank coffee with the Saturday paper
and I didn't get cold until the coffee did
and I needed more. We will plant today

after I dig the sliver out of my toe
seed in the top dress is growing
its beginning. And the sun is warm and
            the top
ground is drying, leaves wilt wanting
            water now

and underneath is ready for roots from
            cell packs-
$2.95 for four, or $3.00 at the church sale
rounded to $20 for charity. See you
            tomorrow.
The lawn needs cutting again.

Choir solo

sometimes bells and smells
mostly bread and baptism
funeral candles empathy choir
thursday night, harmony sunday.

Sometimes dinner with harps
poets sing saturnal waiting
to celebrate very dark
winter. It's snowing.

Joyful noise warms our 'or more
of you' morn processing
the aisle in full color voice
called together cantor

psalms of hope my notes
hold true to the windows.

Ruhn in frieden

The worst thing we ever did was put God in
the sky.
-        Chelan Harkin, "Susceptible to
         Light"

All souls, rest in peace.
Pluck divinity from a dazzling ordinary

choir with no direction, weeks until
            Christmas.
We will sing Schubert's "Litanei"
            on Sunday,
All Hallows' and Remembrance Day this
            viral

year, little goblins out tonight. They treat
their warnings of midnight: spirits
will dance in the dead center of town.

They rehearsed the danse macabre,
drink ghoul-aid, play trombones
but settle down again. Morning, behind
the yews, chimes, "All souls, rest in peace"
but only in an English translation.
German may upset somebody.

Retreat

You were a young man in '57.
I was busy being born.

It will be an A-frame cottage in the forest
reflecting the lake. Decks, windows
catch the light. High and far enough
back the ice won't reach it at break-up
a base in this land as wide as my reach.
And I will have some peace there

on stones and postcards etched
Roblin Mills, upon a bough to sing
what is past, is passing, is to come
mirrors Roblin to its depth.
The fire-place sparks pine sap,
heats the corners, the loft. Kitchen

and bedrooms are down the wing
with blankets for Ondaatje or Atwood.
Cohen on deck, shirt off. Drinks
and dishes provide content; kicked
leaves and gravel roads, words
think as it quiets around tables,

sheaves of revisions in the bush

writing the breeze, beers in bars
not far away, close enough
for a walk, a bit of time.
There are fishing rods
tucked between talk, the lake

stocked trout, and bass. Perhaps a canoe
keel on shore waiting for moments
caught in a line, an image, reflecting
sunrise fades through windows.
Poems and stories begin
with coffee and bacon. Eggs?

Ordinary time

Trilliums are spent. Three
leaves are groundcover.
Seeds germinate. The grass is short
first time this season. Cedar beam

decks, wild rose, clematis purple
gardens trimmed under maples taller
than saplings. They drop keys. Hyacinths
tulips draw into the year. Bearded

iris, begonias, impatiens, lawn
mower red wheelbarrow
black loaded with topsoil.
patio stones with ant nests

hand high shadows creep
branches grey-fired in red light.

The life of trees

when you plant seedlings
you think about next years'

leaves between daffodils
wrestling tulip, wrestling

high as the house
hides private moments

darkened away
stacked in the garage

When towers fall

Ambulance doors close
in the street, hands

legs spread helplessly watch
the drive and nothing but count

out a princess birthday party
in your room, Friday flicks on the player.

I kissed and you. You kissed back
and gone. Even the undertaker cried.

I told the children I was with you
that you loved our arms around, our heads.

Welcome to the world.
Sorry about the mess.

smile and look to me
shudder and ecstasy

sing your worried
grey-green moods

back-lit, wind gold
cradled and skies

roil, rain drives
synchronous tree-bent

cadences and nuzzles
this private crook

kiss goodnight

I opened the door and told her I made
Jimmy Carter's Hawaiian chicken,
confessed I made the recipe up with
peanuts, pineapple, and parents away.

They told me hurry the children
to daycare, come quick
hold her right hand to
time to close her eyes.

Big brown beaver

Big brown beaver builds a dam
builds a lodge for kits, teaches them
play in the forest sharpening teeth
learning tail slaps, having fun.

Big brown beaver tells stories and sing-songs
join the dance in this wub-game
made up today stretching
the edge of this world, then the next.

Big brown beaver teaches canoe:
how to paddle, turn them over
and climb back in ready to bow rivers
and stern rapids and the next

big brown beaver repairs the dam
prepares the lodge for kits
between riverbanks flowing forward
trickles need attention

Hops

Gather ye rose buds...

She yells from the back of the bus,
a sweatshirt she might fit next year

sweatpants with the cuffs rolled up
and my Hebridean hiking shoes.

They fit her now. She hugs me
and I don't want to let go.

She smells happy like camp.
"Let's go dad. I need to do laundry,

have a shower, maybe early
bed and back tomorrow."

Model for single parents

The backyard is a canvas.
You sketch summer and shadow
compost and topsoil and dream
smoothing over shades and water.
Come out. Catch your breath this evening.

She tries her graduation dress
her strapless bra and promises
to bring a shawl. You can't speak.
She is your emerald necklace
and earrings, a smile and perfect eyes.

Ramen bar

a small-town kid in a place you might see
        dragon
things so high you can't help but look up
and there's a ramen bar at the corner.

I put the cover on your mattress, check
the bathroom ceiling, put it on your
        inspection form
take you for a long lunch at the corner

and whisper, "You got this, you got this"
your face your hands hug tears
watching back to your dorm.

An illusion of perfect carpentry

The base is sound. The upper leans
over the clematis climbing up

falling back. Shore the foundation.
More work less cigarettes.

I'm paying for done as soon as you said
you knew about decks and tools, cut

tight 45s and 90s. No gaps screwed though.
I have a friend, a carpenter.

He built houses, stores and banks,
did hardwood for me. He said

buy this stuff for joints, where they don't
quite meet, split posts filled close to perfect

a light sand and paint
each year hides blemishes.

Zen garden no. 4

like a nut buried
ripe with snow dust covering
it cracking open

it's not about that
anymore silent stirs tonight
morning will wake up

my shoulder, there is
a wet nosing me awake
the cat misses you

Taliesin

Lay lime in the shadows,
neutralize the soil for whatever
might grow in exploding shade.

The lawn mower won't start. Fill it.
Check the oil and prime it. Pull
the cord, prime and pull and check

the oil and pull. Well done.
We need seed, or soil and seed
growing patches. We plant hostas.

They grow in rough spots, front first.
Tonight rains on the topsoil the sun
warms starts grass seed and hopes

it grows. I bought this stuff supposed
to grow for anybody. We water. Cardinals
on branches, chickadees grow fat.

Difference

In the dark, it's like fat-rain
almost snow on the windshield
gone at the touch-down light shines off.
Leaves are compost underfoot.

Be careful with your next step.
We have been ready for something
New and tonight it comes
promising every journey

ends in beginnings
fat, rain and flurry, or a first
forget-me-not under a maple
blushes yellow and green

breathes midseason budding
skateboards and snowboards

Joe's store

Joe has a gumball machine on the sidewalk.
One cent. And if you get the little football
instead, you win and come inside for a prize.

The bulb is near empty. About six pennies
and it's mine. First cent- a gumball,
red I think, the second cent is white

then yellow and the football drops in
for a spin into the store. Joe says
I'm a lucky boy. He gives me chocolate.

Taliesin hides his secrets

It's a garbage box for pick up
giggled into the trunk

disassembled pieces, one and one
stripped and sandpaper

edges cured smooth, oiled
left to dry, sanded again

with your gentle hand-finished
secrets at the foot of your bed.

A hornet nest in the barrels

The queen finds a way between barrels
a sheltered place, hollow like a tree trunk.
or an overhang for building cells

and combs and wait to hatch
adults eating silk caps tending
nest and brood, adding out as

needed and cover the nest
except for the enter and exit hole
all summer, until October.

They groom daughters for nuptials
and the males are stupid cool days
sting your neck, fly away and

When the pandemic is over

Museum windows stretch half a mile
down Fifth Avenue. On Sunday afternoon
the street, the square, the steps are milling

filled with women with smiles and blowing
    dresses
old men with canes and wives and families
with New York or Picasso t-shirts and
    baseball caps

sitting, strolling with the sun, listening to
    jazz
bass or renaissance electric lute, watching
mimes and juggling balls. An old man hawks
    beer

pulling cold cans from a shopping cart full
    of ice
buckets while children play, ice cream
    smeared
on faces and musicians play for applause or
    change.

Inside, the old masters wait for Mondays'
    crowd

but here, on the steps the weekend lingers
in sunshine and someone has another
    quarter.

Dog days

The radio says to check the A/C.
Ten degrees difference from outside
is enough for anybody.

Midsummer sweats haze
and sometimes breathes.
Mottled gardens wither

cooler in this spent shade
flowers, grass won't grow
some million indolent things.

Unto Caesar

blistered bare foot
cooling central air
refrigerated bottled
water the power grid
hum each house seeks
rain even just thunder

pile the fire pit low
the spark can be great
tent tree, wide water
framed leaf and needle
star whitecaps sparkle
laughter outstretched

shoulders glistering this
trout and bannock

Rocky

My cough doesn't bother you, does it?
or the way I look, pitch-black in this wool
    coat?
I've been fishing today in the firth, and
    tomorrow
if you're here, I'll give you a present of
    salmon.

I'm not boring you, am I?

I just like to sit with youngsters like you
and have a bit of intelligent talk.
Ah! Manager's watching. He'll think
I'm disturbing his customers. He'll throw me
    out.

I'm not bothering you, am I?

You know, I went to university,
studied medicine here in Edinburgh
but I liked the whisky a bit too much.
I'm not boring you – say and I'll go.

Do I smell bad? I'll go if I'm bothering you.

I had 50p in Ireland once and was going for
    a pint
Just to keep the chill away- I get real cold,
    you know-
saw a little girl with irons- that's not the
    right word-
braces on her legs limping down the road.

That barman will throw me out if I'm
    bothering you.

She stopped and said hello and talked to me
    a bit.
So I bought her a sweet and she kissed me,
kissed my cheek and me soot black.
Her mother saw, screamed I was a dirty old
    man
Set the dog on me.

But that young girl smiled on me
and that's all I wanted.
Made me feel good.
But I didn't have whisky.

Slept in the cemetery last night
fell in a grave and couldn't get out.
Someone saw, thought I was a monster.
I broke my ankle – see how it's swelled?

Faith healer gave me a bead; whisky kills
    pain.
Do you mind if I snag your cigarette butts?
Ah! Manager's coming. I've got to go.
I'll bring a present. We'll talk again.

Carley in Irving

I almost wrote her a love song
but I couldn't find a rhyme
or all-night coffee shop.

Not even a cheap Saturday night dive,
you know, "Just five minutes off
the interstate, ten from the airport."

A place with no regular crowd:
not even at happy hour; not even
a cowboy bar - no suburbs here.

A weekend one-night cheap hotel:
a place out of town businessmen avoid;
a place that loses travel-agents clients

but where do you go when you don't know
where to go and no way to go if you did?
You go to the bar. So I did.

It was dead: salesman from Pizza Fantasy
Boise, Idaho with a woman with a gun
who told me she was a prostitute.

Then there was the piano girl, mirrored
ceiling, and little white reflecting lights.

Her songs, old songs, real old songs

about coffee cup love, canned music.
None of the songs I like. But I did like
the color of her hair you know,

like Texas in January, and something
reminded me of someone
I can't remember.

I almost wrote her a love song
but the scene had me shaken
like my next margarita,

and I couldn't find a rhyme
for Carley in Irving except
slightly unnerving.

In a kiva

you cat-dance priestess worship
I summer devotee wander avenues

dew on our lips, eyelashes, the breeze
toss our hair cuddled close

together in sunrise
rituals ignorant of winter

or perhaps an evening, a café
we laugh and call it a dream

and it is. Our hands wander
through the streets singing

bits of songs we don't know
in an attic room in lace

bending over us I watch
this rose blossom in your eyes.

Around edges

If light crept around edges of drawn   blinds
sharpened the lines of your lips, eye
          lashes
shoulders and curve of your legs it sensed
dreams and fingers and we might have
          only slept.

Desire traced the creases of hands
touched knees mingled breath and breath.
Half-light became the mystery here
shrouding possible expectations, the
          darkness

suggested flesh could be easy, and lies
breathe in the night. But the problem
          could be
our eyes fluttering open on limits
reality defined and happening.

Instead, we waken, pull clothes and shoes on
and know daylight reveals sometimes secret.

Trinity Bay
after Stan Rogers

Careen from masts, dog watching
the sun lift shrouds in inches
as high as the cliffs, the rock
base mists our face.

Whales play in Trinity Bay,
past Doc cove, past the Old Man
beyond it, spout and salute
their flukes out broaching waves

under cliffs above the tree line
high as the fog horns boom away
combers away. Bergs pass God's cove.
We are small on the pitch. They breach

beside our bit of plastic with a motor,
spread fall-back crash-splash another way.
We shiver in float-suits. We wait.
Summer muscles will find Hibernia

rough-neck livings. Black spouts
rise, tails flip high and straight down
full of air for a few good minutes.
Gulls and plovers nest these cliffs.

Puffins on the bob can't fly, their bellies
too full and the tide carries the wharf away.
The town is empty except for tourists.
The post office hopes for letters

that almost never come
but you will come back and mumble,
"See you dad. Paul's in from God's Cove.
Been working the mussels."

Pandemic Hallowe'en

Leaves rain the breeze down
yellow and red for chasing.
Hear them snap and swoop?

They gather in roof gutters,
on sidewalks, on doorsteps
with Jack-o-lanterns.

Most of this season ends
tomorrow - set clocks back
rake leaves - but tonight I see

the blue moon through
skeleted branches
still over cemetery lawns.

I'm ready: candy and chocolate.
My mask says Boo! But there are
no children. Nobody comes.

We pack little grab bags, sweets
left on doorsteps, shouting
trick-or-treat. It was an adventure

when I was eight, and could go around
blocks with friends, dress-up and giggle

no worries unless your bag was grabbed

and your friends took you home, crying
shared their candy, and you
felt like somebody loved you.

Karen

Numbers don't make sense here – 134 but
    no 57
on the right- hand side because the bush has
    taken
the top of the hill. No flooding worries
a ceiling beam 150 years ago. Good bones.
Three cats, a basset hound and wildflowers
prepare for next spring, settling roots

let them grow but find the septic tank.
Roots like septic; septic not so much.
Find out later. You are happy
and we talk our way to sleep.
I'm in your bed on the second floor;
you, in the cat room downstairs.

You tell me to watch the sunrise spectacle
and I rouse to a cat paw on my nose
the sun coming behind deer bush
coyotes and worked-out mines
morning coffee, and hummingbird acres
curled in the place you should be.

Pandemic idyll

It's ok if I dawdle this morning.
I have this afternoon, and after dinner
will be distracted into this evening
and chocolate drops on the way
upstairs, a television in the bedroom
inches covers up to your nose,
hides your eyes, and if you time

the night right and you can delay
morning until someone else makes
coffee. Window light behind
the next fraction of this browsing.
Get the newspaper
on the easy down the outside stairs.
I could go grocery shopping or leave it

to the armchair at the end of the table.
new funnies, a horror-scope every day
and Sudoku, then the front section again.
I'll get to the crossword. Something
makes the time flow slow into more
practiced procrastination.
Afternoon is a distraction, an internet romp

before dinner. Whose turn to cook?

I'll chop veggies if you want.
Did we empty the dishwasher today?
An evening with YouTube videos
news at eleven, drowse into midnight
waiting with empty streets.
Even the church is closed.

Our Lady Seat of Wisdom University
in Barry's Bay

When you drive into the bush, you wonder
if the roads match the map. What about
washouts, or roads with detours only
locals know. Few cottages string the lakes,

stretch forests over hills like a green
blanket with a tiny town on the way
to somewhere no one ever goes with dirt
roads and a steeple everyone close can see.

Downtown is a few stores at the crossroad
a restaurant and the beer store down
where the trees start, closed on Tuesdays.
But cars stop if you want to cross the road.

A fishing boat speaks Polish, drifting
as still as dog-day afternoons.
Our Lady needs help in the pandemic:
they promised first year online and have

nothing in place except this outsider
in a mask with a month before launch.
Air ripples west to east and tonight
will be silent-dark like the stars.

The moon wanes over my cottage
a short walk to school, but everything is.
Deer steal past: two does and a young buck
on watch to sound the alarm if I move.

He waits. The does forage and fade
into the bush. Mosquitoes are free.
He follows into too dark to see
morning with Covid and no coffee.

Kamaniskeg

Slip below dark
scatter clouds reflect
a car pass along shore.
It's an event.

Three is a parade
down hanging orange
edges in the sky grey
patches, stretch-west

back-lit forests ripple
by this hastily pressure
treated deck, hanging
lights and spaced tables

for socially distanced
burgers and fries. My car in front
of my room. The place closed.
Nobody. Nowhere but the door

is open, keys inside
Blue fades loons, the last
ripples smooth in this
silhouette imperial. A car passes.

Campfire cards

We light candles outside, enough
for cards we play with bower
bravado in a lanterned forest
fire steady and low, surrounds

rounds of laughs, a comment,
a lone hand if you feel lucky.
Dead wood feeds burning
hot, building embers

quiet like summer at night
starring as still air breathes
weaved words, wiles passing
this moment and candlelight

shadows. Your eyes are coals.
Your skin is smooth.

Harvest

highways avoid Ontario
filigree porches stain glass
birch and maple farm

antique barn side
vegetable stands full lingering
fields square Erie sun

the black earth market yellow
green been breeze
pepper broccoli zucchini

cutting board knives blanche
beans stewed tomato
steam to the freezer

frost lines quilt windows
pans measure in jars
burners simmer

compliment shaping into
old glass and wine, jokes
made up about cows and sheds

Taliesin in Montreal

Windward sea green
gray tumble sky
atlantic blue lean close
whisper almost touch
lips eyes smile dark
hair windswept
behind one ear

bright flash white red
loud bar crowd drifting
smoke percussion
dancing dark hair
lips eyes smiling almost
fooled to shouting

Storyteller in stop motion
after Ted Hughes

wood crow
orphan outcast
eating squirrel
ragged dirty
scarred in trees

filth covered
they laugh
hold noses
pass heavy
heart crow
forest away

birch shore
canoe crow
kneel paddle
and shoot
over cloud

under moon
river slow
rise canyon
cliff crow
campfire voice

give me corn

night blind
crow still
forest star
burst moon
burn low
crow voice

give me tobacco
you are
my story
I am
satisfied

fire whist
smoke star
morning edge
crow corn meal

black east
and hunt
village crow
fire friends
forest full
crow tobacco
crow bead
story night

fire flicker
deer clothes

and pouches
lodge crow
daughters two
and youngest

done
my pouch
done

and woman

my son
in law
is here

bread crow
bride night
ember glow
crow light
red bride
breath whisper

I sent canoe
to you

crow

scar covered
pelt crow
bird bride
kneel paddle
canoe shoot
forest sing

birch shore
past once
passing hollow
crouch creep cry
rise buck bead
quill pouch

bright sky fire
ring sit crow
bride dance
tobacco needle
crow

here another
edge tale. Hear!

Blueberry war canoe

I Nor'est

Gorse is cold
icebergs drift
nowhere over
down there

grow billows
almost white
brown eyes
week worn

eagles tend
top black spruce
birch nests fly
catchers in camp

let the blueberry
canoe through to the sea

II War canoe

stroke
bare broad backs
stroke

Oh the year was 1778
stroke
how I wish I was in Sherbrooke now

stroke
stop port
stern stroke

paddle-breathe
our blue canoe
and finish for the cameras

Denouement rainbows. Scouts bug out

Winter was joint aches suddenly
seize temperature rise and raises
a thousand tents and almost wish
it wasn't so hot. But it is and we like it.
All-sections: five to eighteen big guys,
dads and leaders and we are here

all of us from all over. I know you
Burl's Creek as cubs or venturers
smuggled screech into camp Nor'west.
We have an extra tent just in case
that storm last night ripped pegs loose

and the fly in the wind collapsed
this free-form afternoon pelting
rain sideways, crowded shelters.
It seems it's been raining
for hours and hours.
Hawkeye says rain

is good for flowers
trees we planted at the reservoir.
Let it pass. It did. It stopped
for a sunscreen sky ready to break

and we laughed the heat away

prepared on a hilltop bowled grey
storm coming. When you think?
Three maybe four hours. We were right.
Cloud curled dark rained vertical
cold. Did you bring gear? Layer up.
As long as the tents don't leak.

They shouldn't. Water clogs screens.
You can sit further back to play cards.
A young one shies from gummies
I offer. His brother takes one, says
I'm a leader. See the scarf?

Hungry for Rain

The bush is dry crunch underfoot.
No fire tonight is the story this sunset
sprinkles start our way to bed.
Hear it- light on the roof, the hot rocks?

It's only a little but the bush
breathes drunk through the tinder.
Loons on the lake, mama and chicks
settle and call. The screens sleep

Sunrise, and forests sound
our weather top, striate down
the low water mark, paddle
scraped, the beached keel.

Butt lake

It's like a tunnel. The danger is great.
Clear the fire pit down. Pile rocks

against the prevailing wind. High
and close keeps the sparks down.

Our tents are tree-framed
lakeshores starred deep

like the trout and these hours
sunburned for morning.

Brule Lake

Last spring, the melt water in Rosswood
rose over its old beaver dam
and started trickling, taking first
leaves still decaying from last fall,
then decay from the fall before,
mud and stronger branches and logs
chewed to size and slapped into place.
It burst. Below Brule turned black
and all the trout died in the silt.

You canoed this route a year ago,
carved a campsite in the bush
and drank its clear water;
canoed again this year, found
low water, two dead lakes. Across
Brule you dig and fill sandbags,

paddle them back, sweat a thousand
paces through the bush, and lay them
where what's left of the dam still stands.
Months from now, the first leaves will fall
will be months before the last snow falls
and melt-water run-off fills the lakes.

You may portage this way again
and drop a hook, anticipating trout.

Unto Caesar

blistered bare foot
cooling central air
refrigerated bottled
water the power grid
hum each house seeks
rain even just thunder

pile the fire pit low
the spark can be great
tent tree, wide water
framed leaf and needle
star whitecaps sparkle
laughter outstretched

shoulders glistering this
trout and bannock breakfast

Rain to Islet

Get your shoes and hiking socks
ready. Short each pack. J-stroke

whirlpools, portages, and wet feet
all of us beach this embankment

with turtle eggshells and the bush
is impathable. Clear the fire

pit piled high. Danger needs
foundations for cooking.

Raise your knife point
here. Press here like this.

Scale tail to fin and the cook
sparks these trees these

stars wide and deep
trout and a few hours

without bears. Sunburned arms,
stretched shoulders reflect

our morning bannock and bass
away and snappers scavenge shore.

Taliesin on Timberwolf

Darkness creeps into camp and there is
            no moon.
Only our occasional words jar the quiet.
Shape shadows in brush as broad as the
            black
and our eyes reach stars beyond fingertips

map light with nods focused on this grey
            rock
beginning to feel cold through our clothes.
Tonight will not sleep but our perception
drowses: everything as safe as care and luck.

Night turns the constellations, raising mists.
In the moment a tree falling in the dark
tears branches, falling hard and echoing
leaves settle back. Sense has already tested

distance; will not calm again in this
silence. Heartbeats swallow stillness.

Tipple Fingers

The fishing boats are coming home.
Shake your hair across the ripple light adrift,
and taut as canvas or rope or a sailor's knot,
a cross, around your open neck. This
          pleasure scents
my skin, your bronze texture. Fingers
whisper.

From step stones and pinecones, drop
          your towel –
bare shoulders, cool sun, no wind.
Toes, first inch, ankle, calf, thighs, creeping
to your core. Arms out and tipple, anticipate
arching water, stroke the channel.

Talisman

Cut hands, damp wood and the smell of
       oiled rope
these summer images are engraved in me.
A day of sunshine is a time of hope
and touch exists beyond memory.

My fingertips are calloused. There is dirt
under my nails and covering rough hands
scratched to the elbow. Rope burns do not
       hurt
but I can feel them in this talisman.

A pebble wrapped in chamois and tied tight
Is passed from one to trusted friend.
Each person holding shares in the sight
and, passed in faith, the vision never ends.

An object grows with everyone it's touched.
You trusted it to me and gave so much.

Taliesin in the sugar bush

When the sun rises over the snow
cover and you sweat in your coat,
tap the sugar, red maple, black
maple fraction of the canopy.

Starch in the roots is sugar
rising over the bores you twist in.
Collect it and sugar down
boiled 40 to 1

steam, stir the depths of trees.
Keep stirring. Boil and stir
and thicken the bring-back
syrup to break the fast.

Sine

there is a way to forget
sunset spikes sparked
our eyes, our bodies

taut like a sailors'
knot around our necks
but I haven't found it

Zen garden no. 5

it's a play lot deal
scrutinize calculate glance
the table round

        coloured chips of glass
        adjusting random patterns
        any shock upsets

sounds vault, walls blend this
cathedral of fire and work
into performance

Taliesin moves out

Even dogs can wander away
when they're ready for themselves.
Take the leftovers from dinner
for tomorrow after the furniture
is down for the night muscle cramps
in beds with sheets or sleeping bags.
You have tomorrow to figure it out
at least for back to work.

I will bring you move-in presents:
a toilet brush, a plunger. You need
paper towels, dish soap, scrubbing
pads and tacos with hot salsa
and back home if you want baby teddy
from grandpa or your summer tires
or your mail- you haven't changed your
         address
and you want to see the cat or even me.

On the death of a red squirrel

At first, I didn't mind your scamper along
soffits on a spring morning with coffee

I assumed you would go away, but you
    didn't
even with a one-way door installed.

When you scratched over my shower
morning my vulnerable became

more blocks, one-way doors. You are out
taking up residence in the garden shed.

I could trap and relocate, but it's October
with no nest; a no food death to winter

or a coyote. A rattrap, a peanut
butter trigger is better.

Counting to thirty

It eased vulnerable
that summer placeless
rippled history spiked down
carved in a grand illusion

there would be a greenhouse
depression glass plates and toast
your fingers and coffee
close as thirty years ago

Homeland

Ebb tide comes to me. This inland age
turns me white and the land turns green.

Land of my youth you have taken my days
and my beautiful strength is passed.

But while the wind raises my last wave
there will not be reproach or enmity

between us; rather, I will sing
our nights, our days, remember?

A ship lays idle: masts, sails
like seagull wings impelling stays
beat staccato, steps unsteady with pigs

chickens squalling and puking, let loose.
Sails fill, snap apposition.
Our rudder whirlpools. Tides roll.

When the land is gone
there is only water, wind
and callouses. Migrant eyes stretch

waves and waves disappear. The prow

drives and days hiss a line
split fast, become converging

cliffs and sand scrapes
our bottom. We wade ashore
as a matter of fact, fall on the rock

and breathe to beat sweat.
Before were only deer and wolves
and gorse. We raise hope and turf

homes, a few sticks for thatch roofs,
cradles. Children and livestock scavenge
vegetables, faggots, fish and fire huddles us.

Last night tore our roofs, ice cover
sunup springs sand gleaming
our waking, our warmer afternoon

skies The fields hint green.
We shape downs to paddocks. Seed
in the ground. Children, hair blazed

evening-red laugh stone shores home.
Tomorrow pricks nostrils drawn west
chanting my nursery rhythms.

The wind is high. It's cold. The sun lows.

Its course is short for me. A long time

you touched my cheeks, yellow now
red like fields in falling light. It is well

for you, land of the flood. Ebb
comes to me, a murmur of ever-young

almost overheard through heart flesh
worn thin. I envy nothing.

Dining tonight

Sometimes it's expected:
cash in an envelope
chocolate in stockings, little toys
even if you are eighty. It's tradition.

Paté and crackers, cheese and red wine
spill just a bit on the table, spot the rug.
You are gracious. You say, "don't worry"
but if I catch this we are intact.

Bring salt, bring a damp towel. I can
scrub it in on my knees. Leave it
and vacuum in the morning,
carpet clean will make this fresh

like this dying light celebrates
with pastry, apple, and sugar

Vigla

Moonshine ouzo, watered white
in a taverna up a mountain
falling into the sea. You smile
broken teeth, weathered eye

gulls suspended white and blue
breeze, squeal the sun going
down Vigla's rock turned ankles,
thistles slope to the sea.

You grab my fingers, rivet
our eyes, confide "Vigla sings
to her children, born and met
her song, her air, her days."

You, in your taverna. I in mine
and snow devils dance in the fields.

For Janet, on her retirement

light as reflecting
everything that snow conveys
speeches and cakes

your voice shakes
occasional tears
hug this beginning

Hot chocolate

Snow influences everything
too deep for on-time
plows clear into driveways four
wheel drive might climb, but I won't.

I'll wait for the snow-blow street
party. It's free and the wind wheels
through edges of garage doors
slowing, stopped now, insulated

sheltered as high as our knees.
Look for the newspaper
in the deep-scape; hot chocolate
when tobogganing gets too deep

and faster than branches
above and snow in the air
in the morning coffee drips
deck rails deep and whiter.

We shovelled the cottage roof

Behind the mounds, the double thick glass
the electric heat, the fire trails into
                morning.
Trees shadow whitescapes; footprints,
                new fall.
From the lake, everything looks immobile.

Our breath hangs in front of us, down
to a fishing hole that will freeze tonight.
We bait hooks and wait lured in a contour
beneath our feet. Our propane stove boils.

Hotdogs keep warm in the chatter
in rounds of coffee someone says
a boy fell through the ice;
was under for like 40 minutes.

They fished him out with poles and
                frogmen.
Cold kept his brain and heart alive.

Storyboard

Scene
>   highway
>   winter snow

Pick-up
>   roll west
>   spin white
>   wheels up

Fade to
>   white
>   wind

Pick-up
>   trailor lights
>   blaze vague
>   breaks slide
>   breathless stop

Fade to
>   white
>   wind

Pick up
>   arms and knees

chest blood
black road
curse first

Fade to

prayer
wind

Derecho

the first we knew it crossed the highway
took the power poles with towers
already down and the cellphone

warning came and we could see it come
taking shopping to the car and before I
		could say
it's going to hit it hit and we slammed
		doors

green-grey and lightning curled a veil down
moving horizontal to where it needed to go
rain and hail as big as a hand blurs
		headlights.

It's spring and the earth
is soft spring leaves and old growth
bears the burst or breaks like roofs

the power down for days leaves the world
to darkness and isolate
candlelight melting refrigerators

birds in trees call tornados
Uxbridge and Ottawa nests
Look- broken shells on the doorstep.

Shopping carts

like Banksy: hunters
clutch spears ready
and shopping carts
quick they will scatter

across the parking lot
and I need one for leaning
waiting and searching
the aisles on and back.

Mum is watching

thump the fence-jump to the oak
budding this short sleeve afternoon
sun and nothing to do runs up
and she lurks, everything safe.
He tastes buds, sweet like spring.
She inches to a tree crotch and look! A first
visit with mum and dad, old enough
come out, stay close, mum takes you

to twigs above the hiding place
to taste a first bud. You like it
enough to explore a branch
maybe better, higher mum
watches you reach branches
you never knew, born in my shed.

To cut or not to cut

The trees create a summer glade
but grass doesn't grow
brown and this mottled
July on the back porch,

a book, a beer- maybe two
in shorts glistening
tanned-arm, white-leg
midsummer afternoons

I have to take down trees
if I want grass and gardens
beautiful small and now
there are considerations.

Taliesin and the green man

Trees and widow-makers shadow
the path to Ptolley Bay.
Keep the buildings up, weed beans,
plant annuals, perennial paths

in pots from the deck to the dock.
Always something – change the water
flow under the foundation, insulate for two
more months. Only you stay in January.

Don't come at night. Roads twist
uneven headlights and animals
run, run deer eyes reflect.
You might stop. Moose eyes don't.

They happen like record high water.
We moved the docks up. No beach.
Years back, my son helped drill
low water anchor holes in the rock

underwater this year. This year
will take forest walks after coffee.
Soil in gullies carried back
bury environmental plumbing

the wood stove in autumn
spring stars tend ice holes
a canoe for your love leaves
in your hair. You set bugs free.

Stones

a moment etched in stone
under branches or hills
rise from the sea

glades and unexpected places
echo the pulse of the earth
thrilled in a dance

sudden as talons strike
the upsurge of air and wings
wheel transcending effortless

Epigraph: Some of the stories

truth is a nut
centre waiting

spring breaks
snows and begins

in the back
your distance

on and on isolate
fragments connect

a bug the monitor
reminds you

spend a day planting
might grow next year

when you don't expect
to all a good night

www.ingramcontent.com/pod-product-compliance
Lightning Source LLC
Chambersburg PA
CBHW052106090426
42741CB00009B/1699